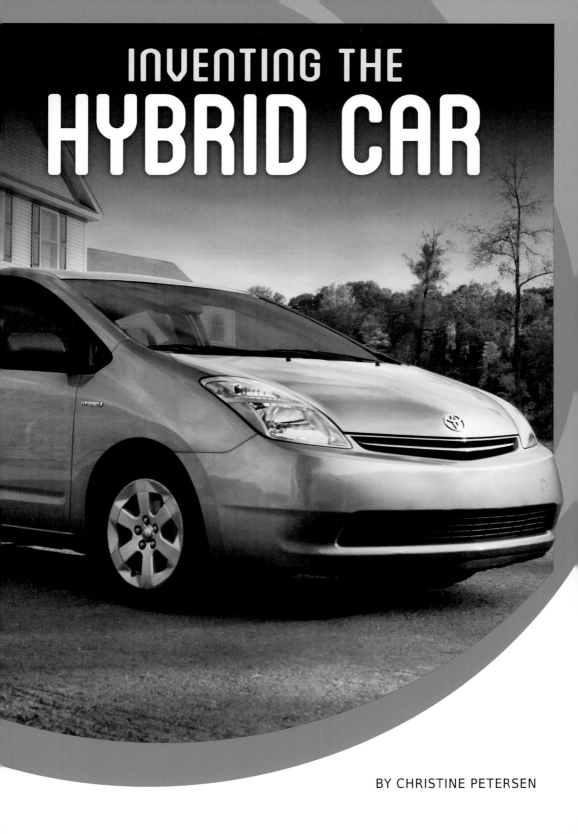

INVENTING THE
HYBRID CAR

BY CHRISTINE PETERSEN

Published by The Child's World®
1980 Lookout Drive • Mankato, MN 56003-1705
800-599-READ • www.childsworld.com

Acknowledgments
The Child's World®: Mary Berendes, Publishing Director
Red Line Editorial: Design, editorial direction, and production
Photographs ©: Owaki/Kulla/Corbis, cover, 1; Bettmann/Corbis, 4, 12; Heritage
Images/Corbis, 7, 8; Michaela Rehle/Reuters/Corbis, 11; Marion Post Wolcott/
Farm Security Administration/Office of War Information/Library of Congress, 14; H.
Armstrong Roberts/ClassicStock/Corbis, 16; Koji Sasahara/AP Images, 18; Dave Alan/
iStockphoto, 20

ISBN: 9781634074568

LCCN: 2015946292

Printed in the United States of America
Mankato, MN
December, 2015
PA02284

ABOUT THE AUTHOR

Before becoming a freelance writer, Christine Petersen enjoyed diverse
careers as a biologist and middle school science teacher. She has published
more than 65 books for young people, covering topics in science, social
studies, and health. Christine is a member of the American Society of
Journalists and Authors.

TABLE OF
CONTENTS

Chapter 1

RACING TOWARD THE FUTURE

On a spring day in 1899, a small crowd gathered along a roadway outside Paris, France. The people talked excitedly as they looked at two cars parked nearby. Cars were not an everyday sight in the late 1800s. Most people still traveled in open carts or boxy carriages pulled by horses. The first automobiles were called horseless carriages because they looked like those familiar vehicles.

But these two cars had a completely different design. They looked more like torpedoes on wheels. Each driver gripped the U-shaped steering wheel. Suddenly a man on the edge of the road raised his hand. When he waved, the cars raced off down the road. Most cars at that time had small engines that could barely manage speeds of 20 miles per hour (32 km/h). That's about as fast as a running horse. So the crowd cheered in surprise when

◄ Camille Jenatzy (left) sits in his car after the race.

Belgian driver Camille Jenatzy zoomed by at 62 miles per hour (100 km/h). No person had ever traveled that fast on land.

Jenatzy called his winning car *Jamais Contente*. The name was French for "Never Satisfied." It was a good description of this man. He worked for years to design newer and faster cars. Some early vehicles used steam to push the engine. Others burned gasoline as fuel. Jenatzy's speedy little car ran on electricity.

Around the same time, German engineer Karl Benz was selling cars that used an internal combustion engine. Gasoline burned inside the engine, providing power to the vehicle. Gasoline-powered cars were not easy to use. The driver had to turn a crank on the hood to start the engine. It was tiring work, and drivers were sometimes injured in the process. But gasoline-powered cars had two big advantages over those using electricity. They were less expensive to build, and they could travel farther.

Early carmakers believed vehicles could be useful to everyone. And they were right. People were tired of relying on horses, which left tons of waste on city streets every day. People also wanted the freedom to travel longer distances in less time. The time was ripe for a new kind of transportation. For a while, the competition was fierce between steam, gasoline, and electric automobiles. Which type of car would finally rule the road?

Karl Benz (right) drives one of his cars in 1893. ▶

Chapter 2

STEAM, GASOLINE, AND ELECTRIC

Cars were a new invention in the late 1800s. But they were not a new idea. More than 400 years earlier, a young artist named Leonardo da Vinci drew plans for a cart that could move on its own. His machine had gears, a steering wheel, and even a brake. Leonardo never built his cart. But he inspired others to believe in the possibility of horseless carriages.

In 1712, inventor Thomas Newcomen created a steam engine that was powerful enough to run machines in mines and factories. Steam engines made work faster and more **efficient**. Two college teachers from the Netherlands took that idea in a new direction. In the 1830s, Sibrandus Stratingh and Christopher Becker built a car with a steam engine. They motored through the streets of their town and into the countryside.

◄ **A man operates a steam-powered vehicle in the mid-1800s.**

The car worked, but its inventors were disappointed. They thought the steam car was too bumpy and noisy. Back in the workshop, Stratingh and Becker had another bright idea. Their next car would run on electricity.

They studied the work of Alessandro Volta, who had found a way to store electricity in batteries. They also read about an electrical motor made by scientist Michael Faraday. Putting it all together, Stratingh and Becker built a three-wheeled vehicle with an electric motor on top.

Their little cart was not sturdy enough for a person to ride. And the battery died after just a few minutes. But the idea caught on. European and American inventors began making tricycles with electric batteries.

In the late 1890s, Ferdinand Porsche was living in Germany. He was thinking of ways to make electric vehicles even better. Gasoline engines sputtered and spat out stinky smoke as they ran. Porsche knew that electric cars were quieter and cleaner. New York City had already put several dozen electric cars on its streets as taxis. Some businesses had replaced their horse-drawn carts with electric delivery trucks. But electric vehicles could run for only a few hours before the battery died. The battery's charge ran out even faster on hilly or rough roads. This limited the distance people could travel.

▲ **Museum visitors look at Ferdinand Porsche's first car.**

Porsche had a brilliant idea. In 1900, he added gasoline-powered engines to one of his cars. The engines fed the electric battery, giving extra power to the car's motor. This new vehicle made less smoke and noise than cars powered by only gasoline. And it could travel farther than cars running on only electricity. Porsche had invented the hybrid car. It ran on both electricity and gasoline. One person called it "the greatest invention of the age."[1] Was this the car of the future?

Chapter 3

THE PROBLEM WITH GASOLINE

When gasoline is burned, it releases a lot of energy. That allows gasoline-powered cars to go faster and farther than cars that run on electricity or steam. Gasoline is a product made from oil. And in the early 1900s, people discovered huge amounts of oil in Texas. With so much oil suddenly available, the price of gasoline was very low.

Henry Ford started a car company in the early 1900s. He began to sell his gasoline-powered Model T car in 1908. The car was "large enough for the family, but small enough for the individual to run and care for," said Ford.[2] And it cost far less than other vehicles. But like all of the early gasoline-powered cars, the Model T was difficult to start. Someone had to turn a hand crank that connected to the engine. It was a miserable job, especially during rain or snow. Four years later, a new type of engine starter

◄ Oil shoots out of a Texas well in the early 1900s.

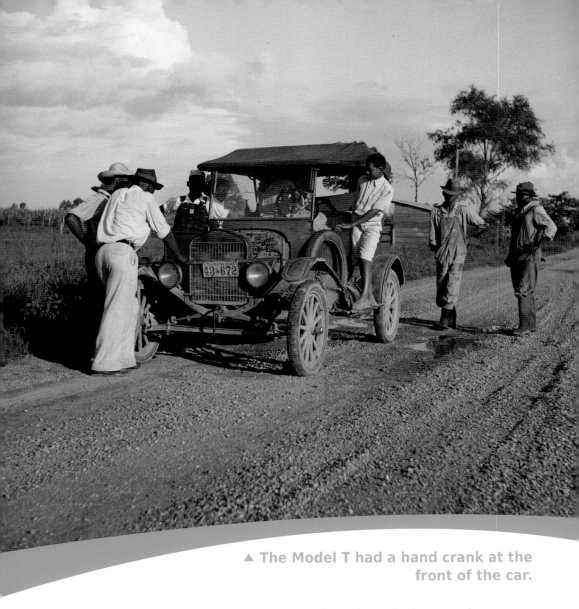

▲ The Model T had a hand crank at the front of the car.

was invented. This starter could do the job with the simple turn of a key. Carmakers paid attention to these trends. They noticed that gasoline-powered cars were becoming more popular. They stopped making electric and steam cars.

Within a few decades, gasoline-powered cars were everywhere. These cars were fun and useful. But they also created problems. In the late 1950s, scientist Charles Keeling started taking measurements of a certain gas in the atmosphere. This gas is called carbon dioxide. Keeling noticed that carbon dioxide levels were increasing. This gas is released when gasoline is burned in an engine.

Carbon dioxide rises high into the sky and builds up around the planet. A high level of carbon dioxide causes our planet to grow warmer. Hybrid cars use less gasoline, so they create less carbon dioxide. That means they do less damage to the environment.

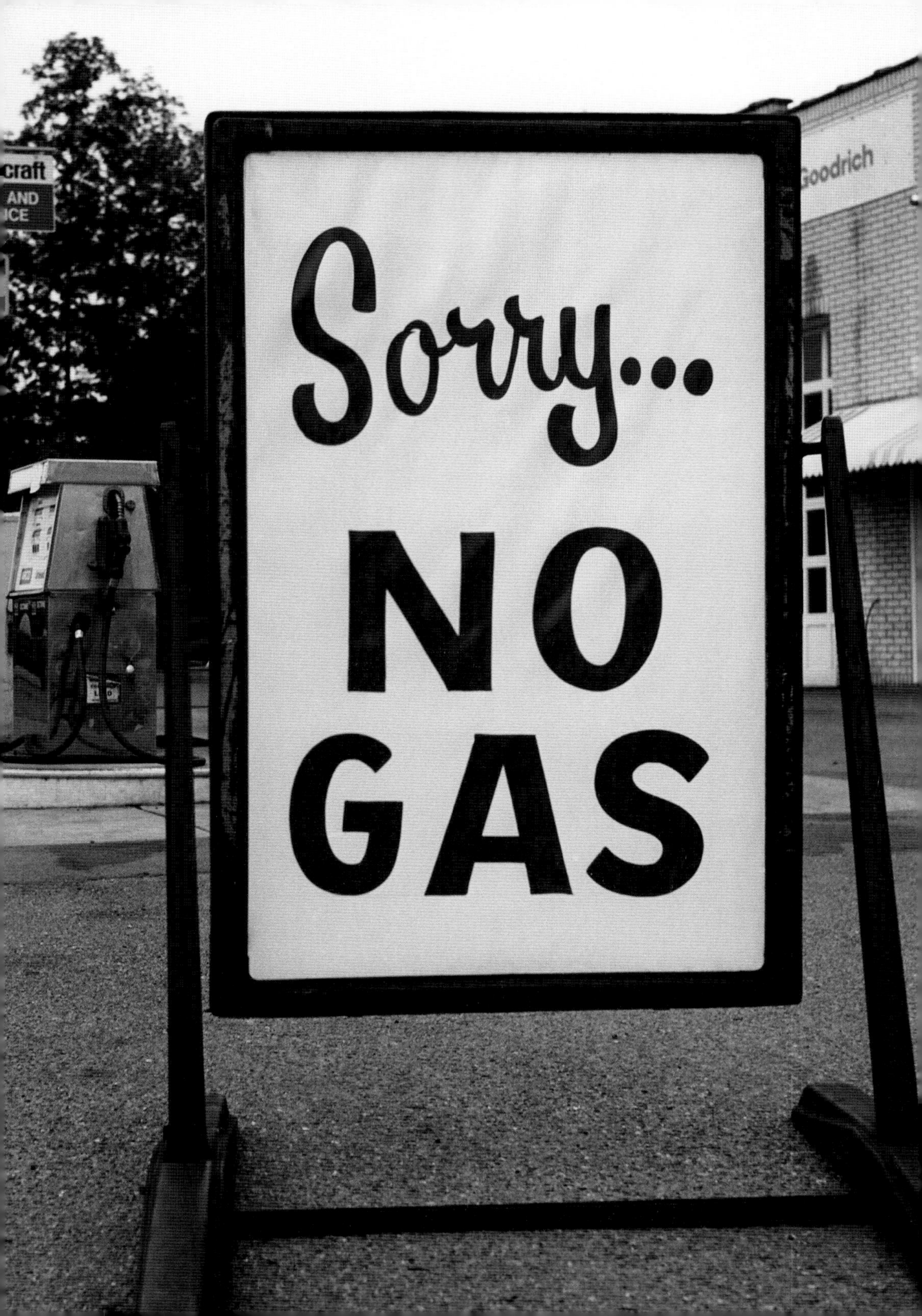
Sorry...
NO
GAS
Goodrich

Chapter 4

A CLEANER CAR

All of Earth's oil formed millions of years ago. Once this oil is used up, it cannot be replaced. There is still a lot of oil in rocks under parts of the United States. The country also buys oil from other places to meet the demand for it. In 1973, the United States was unable to get oil from nations in the Middle East. Oil and gasoline prices skyrocketed. People had to wait in long lines to fill their tanks. And they were not allowed to buy gasoline as often. That shortage reminded people to consider other forms of energy. Some believed that electric or hybrid cars might be the solution.

In 1976, the U.S. government passed a new law. This law encouraged car companies to build electric and hybrid vehicles. The first models were too slow for highway driving. And their batteries held enough charge to drive only 40 miles (64 km). That was not much of an improvement over cars available back in 1900.

For a while, it looked as if hybrid and electric cars would remain nothing more than a dream. Then California gave carmakers a

◄ **In 1973, some filling stations ran out of gasoline.**

reason to keep trying new ideas. In 1990, the state passed a law requiring one-tenth of California's cars to be pollution free.

The Japanese car company Toyota challenged its engineers to design a hybrid car with long-lasting battery power. By 1997, they had done it. Toyota called its new car the Prius. The name is Latin, meaning "to come before." It is a clever reminder that Toyota was the first to make a really useful hybrid car. The president of Toyota said, "The Prius is Toyota's response to the challenge of change."[3]

▲ The Prius went on sale in Japan in 1997. It was available in the United States by 1999.

Thousands of Prius cars were sold in that first year. People signed up months in advance to get one. Today, the Prius and other hybrid cars are a common sight in many places around the world.

Most hybrid cars are **parallel** hybrids. The gasoline engine and electric motor work at the same time to turn the wheels. But a hybrid's gasoline engine shuts down when the car is not moving. So at a stoplight, the car goes silent. First-time hybrid drivers may worry the car has stopped running. But the gasoline engine kicks in again when the driver pushes on the **accelerator** pedal. On the highway, the gasoline engine also helps to recharge the electric battery.

Until the 1990s, most cars were designed with boxy shapes. Air pushed against the windows and slowed the cars down. Drivers had to accelerate or risk losing speed. Accelerating uses more gasoline. Car designers wanted to solve this problem. So they came up with new shapes. Many of today's cars have sleek, rounded shapes. This helps air slip over the top. The new shapes are just another way to improve fuel efficiency.

Designers kept coming up with new ideas to save fuel. Cars such as the Chevrolet Volt and Nissan Leaf are called plug-in hybrids. When the power is running low, owners can plug the car into a household electrical outlet. Its battery will recharge

▲ Plug-in hybrids started to become more common in the mid-2010s.

overnight. Some cities have set up charging stations. Drivers can park and plug in for free to get a quick recharge. There are even smartphone apps to help hybrid drivers locate the nearest public charging station.

Hybrid cars use gasoline engines some of the time. That means these cars are not completely pollution free. To achieve that goal, designers will have to build cars that can use different fuels. One idea is to use fully electric vehicles. So far, only a few car companies have made that switch. And those cars are very expensive. But the designers will not stop thinking of new ideas. Maybe someday cars will run on sunlight, wind, or even waterpower. For now, hybrid cars help the environment by reducing the amount of air pollution.

TIMELINE OF THE HYBRID CAR

1478	Italian artist Leonardo da Vinci draws plans for a cart that can move by itself.
1712	Thomas Newcomen invents the first steam engine.
1834	Dutch teachers Sibrandus Stratingh and Christopher Becker build a cart with an electric motor.
1899	Camille Jenatzy wins a race in his electric car, setting a speed record of 62 miles per hour (100 km/h).
1900	Ferdinand Porsche combines gasoline engines and electric batteries in the same vehicle, inventing the first hybrid car.
1908	Henry Ford begins selling his Model T car, an affordable, gas-powered family car.
1973	The United States is unable to buy oil from countries in the Middle East, inspiring car designers to think about electric cars again.
1997	Japanese carmaker Toyota releases the hybrid Prius.
2014	More than 500,000 hybrid cars are sold in the United States.

GLOSSARY

accelerator (ak-SEL-er-ay-tur): The accelerator is a pedal that the driver presses by foot to make the vehicle go faster. By pushing the accelerator, the driver moves the car forward.

competition (kom-puh-TIH-shun): Competition is the act of trying to do better than others. There was lots of competition between gasoline-powered and electric-powered vehicles.

efficient (ee-FISH-unt): Efficient means using less effort or time. The hybrid car is more efficient than gasoline-powered vehicles because it uses less fuel.

hybrid (HY-brid): A hybrid is a combination of two things. Hybrid cars contain two power sources: a gasoline engine and an electric motor.

internal combustion engine (in-TUR-nul kum-BUS-chun EN-jun): An internal combustion engine burns fuel to provide power to a vehicle or other machine. A gasoline-powered car has an internal combustion engine.

parallel (PAR-uh-lel): Parallel means happening at the same time. A parallel hybrid car has a gasoline engine and an electric motor that work together.

transportation (trans-pur-TAY-shun): Transportation is the act of moving goods or people from one place to another. Cars are the most common form of transportation in the United States.

TO LEARN MORE

Books

Corbett, David. *A History of Cars.* Milwaukee, WI: Gareth Stevens, 2006.

Gifford, Clive. *Cars.* New York: Crabtree, 2013.

Swanson, Jennifer. *How Hybrid Cars Work.* Mankato, MN: The Child's World, 2012.

Web Sites

Visit our Web site for links about hybrid cars:
childsworld.com/links

Note to Parents, Teachers, and Librarians: We routinely verify our Web links to make sure they are safe and active sites. So encourage your readers to check them out!

SOURCE NOTES

1. "LA Auto Show – Porsche's Hybrid Legacy Spans 100 Years." *Porsche*. Porsche Cars North America, n.d. Web. 6 Aug. 2015.

2. Henry Ford. *My Life and Work*. Garden City, NY: Doubleday, 1922. Print. 73.

3. "The Hybrid That Started It All." *Toyota*. Toyota Motor Corporation, Nov. 2008. Web. 6 Aug. 2015.

INDEX